a delicate heart

poetry

by abby jeane

abby jeane/a delicate heart

He held my heart in his hand, and just like glass, it shattered when he dropped it. Throughout the months I picked up the shards of what used to be me, trying to place them together and make something new. Time went on, and the pain started to subside. Though the memory of us still had me shattered, I knew part of me would forever sit in the palm of his hand.

These are poems that describe the stages of heartbreak and my experience with it.

Love is a beautiful but dangerous game, especially because the heart is so _delicate_.

I hope you love this book as much as I do <3
so much love,
abby jeane

This isn't a book about you.
It's a book about me, and how I dealt with losing you.

abby jeane/a delicate heart

contents

Chapter One

intuition.

I *knew* it.

A week before it happened.

I had this terrible feeling, a gut feeling.

The words "breaking up" kept appearing in my mind.

I thought they were just thoughts, that it was just my

anxiety.

Always trust that gut feeling.

The uneasiness in my stomach.

3 times.

It went through my head 3 times that day.

I tried to ignore it.

Tried to tell myself that they were just silly thoughts;

but something inside me knew they weren't.

When you said it, it wasn't what shocked me first.

The shock was that once again,

I was right.

And I hate that I was.

"It's just a dream my love"

No, it wasn't.

It was a sign. I knew it then, and I'm confident now.

Signs.

Weeks leading up to it,

little things popped up.

Videos on Instagram, songs in stores, topics with friends.

Eventually I started to notice it, that they all related to one

another.

It hadn't been brought up or talked about between us at all;

But I already knew.

A gut feeling.

It's crazy the way our intuition works.

How we can sense when something is coming,

especially when it's negative.

I asked you multiple times and each time I was met with the

answer of "we're okay" or "why would you think that?"

You even said it right before it happened.

Looking back it makes me sick.

My thoughts were always right.

Every single time, I was right.

Who would've known that the small thought in
the back of my mind knew exactly how this was about to
play out.

abby jeane/a delicate heart

Chapter Two

mourning.

This is so weird.

I feel like I should be texting him.

That all of this is just some nightmare.

This isn't real, it can't be.

Not <u>us</u>. Not <u>tonight</u>.

I woke up a few times.

I knew it'd be impossible to sleep through the night.

Where's my good morning text?

Where was our call last night?

The more time passes the more I get hit with the reality of it

all.

You gave up on me, after all those time you said you

wouldn't;

And eventually I'll have to accept that.

Lie.

"I have no intention of hurting you"

But you did.

Why?

Did you forget you said that?

Did it just grow old?

And to think I thought you were different.

abby jeane/a delicate heart

I hate you?

I feel like I should hate you right now.

Like I should be cursing your name and destroying your

things.

I just can't though.

Not a bone in my body could ever hate you,

and your things are far too precious to me.

He removed me from his Instagram bio.

What a 21st century thing to say.

Though as sad as it is, it hurt <u>a lot</u>.

It struck me like a bullet, not seeing my face on his page.

It's as if there's an announcement,

"I'm not with her anymore!"

And what makes it worse is that this is just the beginning.

What're you thinking right now?

How do you feel knowing that you broke us?

The lengths I'd go to be inside your brain right now,

hearing your every thought.

I hope you're feeling upset, that you feel heartbroken.

I hope you cried last night and feel like shit right now;

Lord knows I do.

abby jeane/a delicate heart

I always thought *we* had it all.

It was me and you against the world.

I was so certain that nothing, <u>nothing</u>, could break us.

I was sure that, Lord forbid if we ever split,

it would be because of anything except this.

Not because we weren't working.

Not because you stopped trying,

and certainly not because you gave up on me.

Yet here I lay,

5:36 a.m,

Feeling abandoned.

Thoughts.

I've never understood how someone can love an animal so

much, but then abandon it like it's nothing to them.

How a child can carry their favorite toy with them

everywhere, then leave it not even realizing.

How a father can make promises to his wife and children,

then leave.

Anyone can agree that all three of these situations are

heartbreaking.

What's even worse is just as that person, child, and father,

You left me.

abby jeane/a delicate heart

Nothing is worse than lying here.

Hoping that something will change,

that it'll all be different.

But this is the change.

<u>This</u> is what's different.

Grey skies.

I always felt that if we were to ever break up,

it would be on a gloomy day.

That if we were to ever split,

the world around me would be sad as well.

I always thought that these were just thoughts;

Yet here I am in the reality of it.

The gloom and the rain.

The heartbroken world around me;

Mourning us.

On my side.

It's so good to know that the universe is mourning us with
me.

How the rain washes the path where you broke my heart
and makes the world around you depressing.

You can try to run, you can try to distract yourself with
family.

Eventually you'll wake up and see the truth;

My memory is everywhere.

abby jeane/a delicate heart

My tears are like the rain.

Effortlessly falling, sometimes hard and sometimes light,

but effortlessly beautiful.

A rainy sky, all over this town of ours.

Everything you love and have, soaked with my sadness.

Can you feel it?

Can you feel the same ache I have in my chest in yours?

I hope you're thinking of me to the rain,

for it is a reminder that you broke the heart of the only

girl you've ever truly loved;

And she falls with such beauty.

Happy birthday my love.

I hate that it's rainy today.

It's your birthday and you love the rain,

but maybe you don't today?

Maybe the rain is a sign of our loss today,

a reminder of what's broken.

I hope that you miss me today.

I hope my name doesn't leave your mind.

I hope that when you make your stupid birthday wish,

You wish to have me back.

My birthday wish for him.

I wish this didn't happen.

I hate that we've split.

I hate that I'm at home crying instead of celebrating with
you.

We could be holding hands, laughing right now.

Enjoying your family and the museum, a wonderful day.

Staring at each other's smiles in a coffee shop.

Instead I sit in my car, alone.

Crying and watching the rain run down my windshield;

Missing you.

Where'd it go wrong?

We used to be so good.

We used to have something so wonderful.

I always thought that it was you and me against the world;

But then you gave up on me, on us.

Right when I was finally feeling confident you wouldn't.

Just a nap.

I took a nap on the couch today.

I felt so upset it exhausted me, so I finally did something
about it.

When I woke up, I expected to see a text from you.

I was certain there'd be one until I remembered the reality
I'm living.

Just for a second though,

It felt like it was just a scary dream.

abby jeane/a delicate heart

And suddenly,

That ache in my chest was back.

Taylor Swift.

I hope you think of me to Taylor Swift.

I hope that when you hear *Lover*,

you think of how we danced in your room.

When you hear *Superman*, you think of how I sang it on the

way home from the zoo.

Whenever you pick up your guitar, you flashback to when

you first played *Nothing New* for me.

That when anyone mentions her name it's my face in your

mind.

<u>My</u> smile, <u>my</u> voice, <u>me</u>.

An eternity just for me.

The songs you'd play and the poems you'd write.

The confidence in your voice when you'd say us being

together just felt right.

Those words that I held onto like life or death, that I can't

remove from my mind,

I should've known it was only a matter of time.

My bedroom.

It's most depressing here.

Lying here, the sunlight that peaks through the clouds

shines through my blinds.

Silence.

Only the faint sound of the tv and the outside world,

and the loud echoing of my thoughts.

I can't call you, can't text you, and I won't see you today.

This is more depressing than when I'm crying my eyes out

and talking about it.

Because in this moment,

I'm just numb.

Your playlist.

"Abstract change"... is that about me?

Or is it about you?

A playlist reminding you that you broke us and now you feel

regret.

I agree, for this is an abstract change.

The most abstract thing about it?

It was <u>you</u> that left.

Our song.

All our songs have a depressing glaze over them now.

Instead of tears of joy, I shed tears of sadness.

The sound of your voice and that look on your face,

forever engraved in mind.

The park.

I was missing you today, so I went to that sweet little park of ours.

I know this area well.

I flashback and remember when we would walk around for hours, talking and enjoying life together.

A part of me expected you to be here, but of course you weren't.

I miss you; please let me back in.

Our old spot.

The bench where you held me that summer night

The swings that I always thought were so fun

The grass where we'd sit and talk, jazz playing from your

phone

The bridge where we took prom photos with friends

This place is so special to me, it holds so many memories of

us

Being here now, I already feel closer to you

I missed this

Our playlist.

A playlist that belonged to us is now a playlist that belongs

to me.

Much like my heart, you came in and added your own

excitement and wonder... then left.

Your favorite melodies all around,

leaving me with parts of you I can never forget.

It's like he died.

The walk doesn't feel the same without you next to me

The leaves don't fall the same, the sky doesn't glow anymore

Everything is just as it was, but it feels empty

It feels cold

This place was for us

Now that you've gone I recognize it in the most unfamiliar,

heart shattering way

I've been here so many times, but it feels different

I keep expecting to see you,

that you'll walk up behind me and tap my shoulder

I can see you now, I can hear your voice so clearly

It's all in my head though

You won't come by

You're gone

I need to accept that

abby jeane/a delicate heart

"I'm doing good, I've come to peace with it"
 It's what I keep telling those who ask.
Yet here I am, in the park we used to go to,
writing poetry about you.
So am I really okay?

The walk.

The walk feels lonely without you.

I hate that I stayed on my side, that I walked on our path.

I found that the tree I posed you in front of has died,

much like our love.

I keep looking around, hoping that I'll see you,

but you aren't around.

And maybe it's for the best.

abby jeane/a delicate heart

What happened to us?

Not that long ago we were here,

happy and in love.

Picturing a future for us, excited to grow together.

It may sound silly and desperate,

but if you told me you wanted that back,

I'd agree.

abby jeane/a delicate heart

I'll wait for you;

Forever if I have to.

You're worth it to me.

Hopefully I'm worth it to you.

Where are you?

I wonder where you are.

Are you at home?

Are you close to me now?

Do you feel an emptiness in your life?

A void that was meant to be filled by me.

I have so many questions, but I never get answers.

Maybe I shouldn't be here, it probably isn't good for me.

I don't want to go though.

This is the closest I've felt to you all week.

Questions.

Have you driven home from work crying?

Have you just laid in your bed in the dark and the silence,

staring at your ceiling with tears in your eyes?

Have I been the first thing on your mind every morning?

Is it hard for you to get through the day?

Do you feel bad about what you did?

What did you tell your family and what do they think?

Have you wanted to reach out?

Do you miss me?

Are you allowing yourself to feel hurt or are you bottling

everything up?

Did you miss me on your birthday as you blew out your

candles?

It kills me that I'll never get answers.

abby jeane/a delicate heart

Your mom's post came on my feed.

Just a picture of you, smiling.

The picture was old, I'd seen it before;

But God, did that hurt like hell to see.

The mall.

The mall makes me think of you.

All the stores we'd go into, the way you'd criticize clothes in

the most obnoxious but hilarious way.

The food court, we had our first date here.

Do you remember how magical that Thursday was?

How we shared laughs and exchanged poetry.

The last time we were here, we were with your mom.

She bought me that little red gnome that now sits on my

desk.

I would have never guessed that would be our last trip here

together.

His annoying opinion...I kinda like it.

When I see clothing I think is cute,

I expect you to quickly say "no it's not" as you put it back

on the shelf and gently push me away.

Then I thought it was funny and annoying,

but right now I miss that more than ever.

Oh what I would do to have you say that just one more

time.

The food court.

Sitting in a crowded room, I look around.

Glancing at all the different people around me,

all smiling and excited for the season.

I can't help but think I'm the only one in this room that's

sad, that's heartbroken.

That's so selfish of me to say, but it feels true.

I mean, who gets broken up with a week before Christmas?

Everything reminds me of him.

I can't go to certain places because we used to go together.

I can't eat certain foods because we'd always get it together.

I can't listen to certain songs because those were our songs.

I can't bring myself to do all these things because they

remind me of you and the memories that we made;

And it hurts to do them knowing that you're gone.

abby jeane/a delicate heart

Are you thinking about me?

Because I'm thinking about you,

For you are all that is on my mind.

Shocked faces.

Everyone I've told thought that I was lying.

Did you get that same reaction?

The shocked faces of loved ones, covering their mouths and

gasping.

And it just breaks my heart to see that, for it shows

that everyone who knew us thought that we'd be endgame.

Every. Single. Person.

9:23 a.m.

This is the longest I've slept in days,

Yet I still wake with you on my mind.

He had an open mind for a little while, didn't he?

You told me you never believed in 'meant to be'.

You didn't believe in soulmates.

That you had never had a connection that made it seem true
to you; but then ours did.

Do you remember when you told me you truly believed we
were meant to be?

That was something you had never felt before.

Do you remember when your own mother said we were
meant to be?

When your sister told you that something about us "just
made sense"?

I doubt you believe in any of that now, but if you do,

I know it's because of the connection you had with me.

When your view changed.

There was a girl who made you see things differently.

A girl who changed your rational views on meant to be and

soulmate energy.

A girl who helped you discover so much about yourself,

who was proud to watch you grow.

A girl who loved you for you and all that came with that.

You gave up on her.

How could you ever give up on someone who made you see

life in such a wonderful way?

That's something that I'll never understand.

And something I hope you <u>always</u> regret.

My sweater.

The sweater that he said I looked beautiful in is the same

sweater that he broke my heart in.

The jacket that matched mine is the same jacket he wore

as he walked away from all we had built.

The girl that he wrote poems for, protected,

and loved deeper than anyone else,

is the same girl he's now removed from his life.

My journal.

Since I was 12, I've kept a little journal.

For the last 6 years, I've written every single thought and feeling I've had.

When I met you, I introduced your name to my pen and paper, the same way I had with the previous boys I'd sent my heart to.

Weeks of excitement grew into months, and eventually a year; your name on the paper every night.

I read them to you; my precious, sacred, silly little entries.

You were always on the page, my books being filled with your name.

Now I weep as I continue to write your name, struggling to admit that just like the other boys, your chapter has come to a close.

abby jeane/a delicate heart

I love seeing the excitement in other's faces

when I tell them that we've split.

It hasn't been many, but it feels so good to know that even

though you don't want me,

there's other people that do.

Used to this.

Breaking hearts is something I'm sure you've grown used to.

Your sister once said that you'd be a heartbreaker once you

were grown, and she was right.

I'm not the first girl who's heart you've sliced,

but I hope that I was the first that you felt terrible about.

I miss you.

I miss the way you held me and I miss the way you'd smell.

I miss you calling me every night.

I miss that you always made everything feel just right.

I miss the way we'd kiss, how we would intimately lock lips.

I miss you being my best friend,

and I really miss the feeling that we were never going to end.

Your family.

I miss the way your mom would laugh

and your sister would smile.

I miss the way your dad would talk to me

when he hadn't seen me in a while.

I miss the way you'd mention your brother,

or how you'd say you were just like your mother.

I miss your sweet home that sits at the end of the street,

with all the little nick nacks I always thought were so neat.

It's sad to say that I haven't been over in a while,

but I'll always remember that when I was there,

I would leave with a smile.

abby jeane/a delicate heart

Your loft.

I used to complain about sitting on your couch

and doing nothing for hours

but now I would do anything to go back there.

I would hate when we would just sit there

playing games all day everyday

but now that is the only thing I want to do.

Don't get me wrong, I loved spending time together.

That loft that you liked to call an "extension to your room"

was one of my favorite places to be,

but we spent everyday there and sometimes it felt dull and

overused.

Now I sit at home and look at the time, wishing I was

upstairs in that loft.

Lying comfortably in your arms, playing games all day

everyday.

The coffee shop next to the bakery.

I keep looking into your window and out of ours.

I was sure I'd see your car this morning, but I still haven't.

Are you even going in today? Is it just not till later?

I need to stop, I should be focused on my work, not yours;

But I can't.

I saw a car I thought was yours and felt my heart stop.

Every person I see walking up I quickly scan to see if it's you.

I keep looking over at your coworkers,

Wondering what you think of them.

Even writing this I can't keep my eyes down.

Continuously searching the whole parking lot with hope I
see you.

Though a part of me worries that if I see you now,

It'll break me all over again.

The bakery next to the coffee shop.

It's not a secret I was distracted at work today.

Constantly peering out the windows,

I waited to see you walk up to the little coffee shop;

But you never came.

Honestly distracted is an understatement.

My eyes were <u>glued</u> to the window and the people who

would pass by.

None made me nervous the way you would.

Uninvited.

11:30 a.m.

I got a call and for a second I thought it could be you.

My stomach sank as he told me he talked to you.

Apparently you're not doing well.

You're hurting and seeing me would be too much right now.

It makes me feel better to know that it's killing you

the way it's already murdered me,

But let's not forget who left.

abby jeane/a delicate heart

It's sad to see what we've become.

Where's that man that weathered my storm

and lit my fire in the bitter cold?

The last time we spoke, I didn't even recognize you.

Do you even recognize yourself?

Just know that when you're ready,

I'll be here.

I hate to hate you.

I want to hate you

Honestly I should.

You've taken so much from me,

and I've gotten all the consequences as if this is all my fault.

Yet everytime I say something mean, it feels wrong.

You've created such a shitty situation,

and I still don't hate you for it.

And I hate that I can't.

I don't think I'll ever get over you.

I want to say that I'm over you, but let's be honest.

If I saw you walk into the room my heart would jump.

If I heard your voice calling my name,

I'd run right back home.

If you asked to pick me up, I'd be outside waiting.

I want to say that I'm over you,

but I really don't think I ever will be.

Urges.

Do you have urges to text me?

When you're going out or when you get home,

do you ever think "I should text her"?

I know I do.

It comes and goes, and sometimes I almost do.

Then I flashback to reality,

and I remember what's happened to us.

Staring at the ceiling.

Sometimes when I can't sleep,

I lie here and wonder what we'll be one day.

Friends?

Lovers?

Strangers?

Only heaven knows, and that kills me.

Phrase of sight.

"Out of sight out of mind" is what they say

I used to agree with that little saying

I never thought much of it

Now I couldn't disagree with it more

You're out of sight, but you're all over my mind

When you're ready.

When you're ready to talk, I'll be here.

When you're ready to see me, I'll be there.

When you're ready to mend what's broken,

just let me know.

You're worth the wait, and if you were to come back,

I'd never let you go.

I wish.

I wish your car would pull up in front of my house right
now.

I wish my phone would ring with a call from you.

I wish my mom would come into my room telling me you're
here.

And I wish, I really really wish,

that these wishes would just come true.

Your story.

You never post on Instagram, but you did tonight.

Maybe it's because you wanted to show off that picture he

took of you, or maybe it's because you wanted me to see.

A way of telling me you've been seeing everything I post,

and you can do the same.

Maybe it's one, maybe it's both.

Maybe you didn't even think of me as you hit send.

Whatever it is, I watched that story over and over again;

Missing you more every time.

abby jeane/a delicate heart

Friday night you told me you loved me so much,

that you were so happy you got to see me.

Two days after that you said we could never work.

???

I just don't understand.

How could someone go from being excited about a person

to not wanting them around anymore in the span of 48

hours?

That's something that will <u>never</u> make sense to me.

Why I don't reach out.

I don't reach out and it's not because I don't care.

It's not because I'm scared.

It's not because I've moved on,

and it's definitely not because I haven't given you a thought

since.

I don't reach out because you've made it clear

that you don't want to talk to me,

and I'm willing to respect that.

One day, you'll be ready.

And when you are,

You know where to find me.

abby jeane/a delicate heart

Sometimes I just sit in my room in the dark.

Listening to music, while thinking about you.

And I <u>really</u> hope you do the same.

His ghost.

I hate how easy it is for me to still see you here,

walking beside me.

I hate how vividly I can hear your voice

or your laugh after you would tease me.

And what I hate most of all is that I'm here at our spot,

alone;

And you're not coming.

abby jeane/a delicate heart

Sometimes I have the feeling that I should go to you.

I never know if it's just me, or if it's a prophecy.

I worry that if I actually do it,

you'll be upset with me again.

But then I hope that if I do,

you'll tell me you'd been waiting for this day.

Another poem about how I miss him.

I miss everything about you.

I miss your smile, I miss your voice.

I miss the way you'd laugh when I said something that

threw you off but you found it hilarious.

I miss how you'd tell me you loved me and how you'd kiss

me after.

I miss everything about you.

I want my best friend back.

Please just come back.

abby jeane/a delicate heart

And as I laid there I knew,

he had utterly destroyed me.

And I hated that.

abby jeane/a delicate heart

And it sucks because at the end of the day,

Only <u>you</u> really understand how it feels right now.

Rest in peace, 2022-2023

There's nothing worse than mourning the death of a person
who's still alive.

You don't see them anymore, but you feel them everywhere.

You miss them and crave just one more conversation,

but it never comes.

You can feel time pass as the days bleed into weeks,

but you're still right where they left you,

constantly reliving that last moment with them.

Such an awful, heart wrenching moment to go back to,

but wanting to relive it just to see them one last time.

There's nothing worse than mourning someone who hasn't
died yet.

The only thing that died was your connection,

and the person that you used to be.

abby jeane/a delicate heart

I never knew how much I loved you until
you broke my heart and I didn't hate you.

Young love.

Everyone tells me I shouldn't be so upset

"He just wasn't the one"

That's the thing though

I wanted him to be

I wanted him to be <u>so</u> bad.

It's been three weeks.

Three weeks, such a long but short time.

When I think about it, it only partially makes sense.

Of course it's only been three weeks,

I can still remember every detail so vividly.

But then again, it's been three weeks

and still I can remember it all so vividly.

11:31 p.m

It's weird but I can't help but feel that I'm on his mind too.

That he's also grieving and reflecting on us;

Missing me.

I like to think he's thinking about me.

Is it crazy of me to say that I feel connected to you

somehow?

Like something inside me just knows that I'm on your mind

too.

Maybe it's just the last bit of hope I still have,

but I really feel like you're thinking of me right now.

Missing me, feeling connected to me the same way I feel

towards you,

And that makes me really happy.

Twin flame connection.

Late at night when the house is all quiet and dark,

I get this intense feeling throughout my body.

The kind of feeling you get when you feel truly connected to

someone.

I like to believe that this feeling is because you're thinking

about me.

That once the night dwells upon us and you're left alone,

My image fills your mind.

You lie there, missing me most during a time when you can

just sit and think.

Maybe it's because we are connected,

or maybe I just miss you a lot and need to go to bed.

Tragic love story.

Two lovers have become two strangers.

Mysteries to the world they shut themselves down,

refusing to speak.

Their thoughts immersed in the memory of them,

and the curiosity of what they would one day be.

Two strangers who hold the key to each other's heart,

and the baggage of each other's secrets.

Time around them stands still in the storm of regret and

broken promises.

Days bleed into nights as another day passes without a text

or a call.

Two strangers who used to be deeply in love have vanished

from each other's life.

This is the most heartbreaking story anyone could write,

and we *were* chosen to play it out;

After all those times you promised we wouldn't.

The stars.

Do you ever look up at the sky and admire the stars?

These beautiful balls of light that shine in the night sky,

looking down on us.

As I admire them, I think of you.

The poems you used to write and the way we'd admire them

together.

How you used to call me your moon and stars.

The time we saw a shooting star and I was confident it was

fate.

Now that you've left, I look up alone and wish you'll come

back.

That one day it can be you and I, staring at the sky;

Wishing together.

At least we're still under the same sky.

Jan 2024.

Today marks a month since we broke up.

A month without your texts or calls.

A month without your kisses or hugs.

A month without you in my life.

There's peace in your absence now, but it's mixed in with the pain that will always be there.

Sometimes I wish things were different, but then I look at this for what it is and I remember why it's over.

I've come to accept that I'm moving on and letting go, but I've also accepted that nothing could ever fill your presence.

I could never fill the void you left with someone else, it just wouldn't be the same.

That's not me saying I'll never find someone else.

It's me admitting that I'll always feel strongly for you.

There will always be a part of me waiting to love you again;

whether you come back or not.

Morning notifications.

The hardest part of my day is when I first wake up.

I check my phone and your name isn't part of the list;

and I know that I need to live another day without you.

It's funny when other guys text me thinking they have a
chance.

We'll go out and they'll find little ways to touch me.

Flattering but they don't realize they're talking to the girl
who's still in love with her ex-boyfriend.

No one stands a chance as long as you're still in my heart.

abby jeane/a delicate heart

I gave you the most sacred parts of myself

My body, my soul, my heart

Now I'm supposed to go off and live a life where the boy

who knows me inside and out doesn't exist

Rainy Saturday morning.

Red shirt, coffee bar.

I watch you from afar.

Curious if you noticed me,

hurts that I'm someone you don't want to see.

Two cars, parallel.

Seeing you is a new hell.

One boy, one girl.

Two strangers who once made each other's heart swirl.

Heaven knows we'll never be the same,

So I'll just break inside anytime someone mentions your

name.

A healing heart.

Recently it's felt like I've moved on.

I look at pictures of you and it doesn't feel the same.

I can talk and think about you without ripping my heart
out.

But still every night, I dream of you & I.

I have conversations with the mirror as if we're meeting
for the first time since that night.

I wonder if you'd answer if I called today.

It feels like I'm moving on, but I'm still doing all these
things.

And that's when I return to the question of if I'll ever
actually be able to move on from this,

And I worry I won't.

An old melody.

My relationship with you has faded like an old favorite song.

A beautiful melody I would play everyday is no longer in my

daily shuffle of songs.

I listen whenever it shows up on a random playlist every

now and then, but I don't really remember the lyrics.

It's still very familiar.

If you asked me I'd tell you I <u>loved</u> that song.

I still remember how happy I'd feel when it would play

and how for a while it was the only song I ever wanted to

listen to because I thought it was the most perfect work of

art.

Now it no longer sounds that way, it sounds different.

I can't sing along because I'm no longer confident in the

lyrics that come next.

Watching the music video makes me sad because the magic I

once felt is gone.

An old melody.

My favorite song is no longer my favorite song,

but if you asked me what it is it would be the first song I'd

think of.

And the worst part is that my favorite song is a song I no

longer want to hear.

I hate when it plays unexpectedly.

I hate when my playlist sends it through a random shuffle

mix.

And I hate that my favorite song is now someone else's

favorite song;

and she gets to listen and dance everyday.

My best friend.

Without her I'd be lost

The one person who's gotten me through it

Who's understanding and sympathetic

Who lets me talk until her ears bleed and even then, lets me

continue

She sees it for what it is and she's honest with what she sees

She guides me back to the light when it gets dark and starts

the fire when it gets cold

Without her, I'm not sure what I'd do

I'll be thankful until the day I die and long after that for

what she's done for me recently

For no one loved me the way she did

And I am healed because of her

Ghost of us.

I wonder if he knows he's going to break her.

I swear I'm living a life that's haunted.

I see them walking around everywhere.

The park, the mall, the pizza place.

It's like they follow me.

I even see them around my own house.

I watch as they hold hands and talk, laughing and living life
together.

I've seen them kiss, and I've seen them dance.

I hear him making promises to her, and I wonder if he
knows he won't keep them.

Nothing lasts forever, do they know that?

If I told them now, would they believe me?

Does he know it'll be him that leaves?

Such a tragic thing, watching these two fall in love
just for it to end the way that it will.

I once heard her say, "but he would never block me out if we
ended"

Ghost of us.

Does she really believe that?

Does she even know him at all?

It's so obvious she's lovestruck.

She's never going to be prepared for what he'll soon do, and she'll have to live with it.

As for him, he'll do what he does best and disappear.

He'll shut out the world and run away from a mess he's made, fully aware that he's hurt her and fully unaware that this will force her to see life in ways she never has before.

I truly do feel sorry for these two.

I feel their loss so heavily in my chest, and it frightens me that I don't have the answer of what happens to them next.

Only time will tell.

10 minutes later.

I wonder how you were comforted once you got home.

Did their faces reflect sorrow?

I'm sure they instantly asked why and what happened.

Your mom, being the loving woman she is,

probably embraced you, and I wonder if you cried in her

arms.

What did your sister think? She was always so kind towards

me.

I wonder what your dad said.

After all, he had seen me as the best girl you'd ever brought

home.

What about your brother? He had just returned home two

days prior.

How did the rest of your night play out?

You went to dinner, and even though you were physically

present, I'm sure you weren't mentally there.

I saw you went on a walk once you got home.

10 minutes later.

Since that night I've wondered what went through your head.

You would always go on walks when you had a lot to think about.

I wonder if you cried or if you felt relief that it was finally over.

And what I wonder more than anything is if you remember it all the same way I do.

abby jeane/a delicate heart

That night haunts me.

Over and over again I hear my screams

and see that look on your face.

I hang my head in my hands as the memory of us comes over

me like a random chill, hitting every part of my body,

making me shake.

Till forever.

Don't believe him when he says he'll love you that long.

He said it to her, he said it to me, and I'm sure he says it to

you now.

Don't trust it.

The nature center.

I found myself outdoors, escaping suburbia yet unable to
escape the memory of you.
I walked around and the air felt clean,
but my thoughts were messy.
We were supposed to come here with your family
but never did.
All of it reminded me of you.
I saw a red-tailed hawk and told the story of when we saw
one together.
I saw rocks and wondered how your geography class went.
As I looked at the exhibits I thought about you being a
biology major, and how I'm so proud of you for that.
The whole time I kept thinking, "he would love this"
and it made me sad I was unable to tell you about it or even
have you there.
If only you knew how much I wanted you there.

</3.

Oh how wonderful it would be to hear your muffled voice

saying my name

Flutter my eyes open

And see you looking over at me

Lying on your couch

Like it was all just a bad dream

Up & down.

I wish I could write you a poem that says all that
I want to say exactly how I want to say it, but I can't.
I could never do that because then I'd be writing
forever and it would feel messy.
It would change everyday too.
One minute I'd be telling you how I miss you and
the next I'd be saying that we really are better off apart.
I couldn't write you a poem that says exactly how I feel
because half the time, I don't even know how I feel.
It's something that I look past, I don't want to make it that
deep.
In reality though I know my feelings towards you
are a see-saw sort of experience.
One minute I'll be on a high and then the lowest of lows,
and I've accepted that this will always be how it is.

Maybe those new glasses will help you

finally see the mess you've made.

Delusional little me.

This is crazy of me to think,

But I really think you could be talking to me through music.

I go through your playlists and surmise

that those songs remind you of us.

It might be crazy but I don't think

you're making <u>these</u> playlists with <u>these</u> songs just

because you find them catchy, but more because they're

something you relate to.

I feel silly writing this and I'm sure you'd think it's weird if

you knew, but I think I just might be onto something with

this silly little thought of mine.

abby jeane/a delicate heart

And as he dropped me off and the rain fell

I walked up to my door and all I could think was,

"but he's not him"

And that's what really hurt

I've been thinking.

You probably think that you're stronger than me

because you were the one that left.

But I chose to believe that I'm the stronger one

because I was willing to stay.

Does no one remember?

It's crazy how when you break up with someone,

everyone around you starts acting differently.

It feels like I'm the only person who remembers what we

had.

How can your friends hang out with me like they aren't the

reason we ever met?

How can your family talk to me like they didn't love having

me come around?

How can you live your life and act like I wasn't imprinted

into every last aspect of it?

I feel like I'm losing it.

Does no one fucking remember how in love we were!?!?!

I'd choose you.

In a room full of everyone I've ever loved,

I'd go to you.

In a world of new opportunities,

I'd go to you.

If I was given the chance to have one thing

from the list of everything I've ever wanted,

I'd choose you.

And I hope you'd choose me.

abby jeane/a delicate heart

And with the passing of the rain,

2 months came

I slept alone,

Missing your heart that I once owned

A smile I used to raise

and a love we used to praise

All gone and left to the past

Trying to move on and ignore the silence,

So loud and vast

Reflecting on your words,

and pondering on why they still hurt

The memory of you, revolving in my universe

What used to be my greatest blessing now feels like a curse

Wish this would all just go away

But for two years in heaven,

It's the price I must pay

Falling.

They don't call it "falling" in love for nothing.

The beginning is surreal.

Butterflies in your stomach and stars in your eyes.

You take the leap and you're falling.

At first it feels scary, the unknown of it all.

Ghosts from the past haunting the back of your mind.

But after that first leap, it feels like flying.

You feel so free and alive.

The adrenaline runs throughout your body,

And the air feels so light.

Time goes on and you get closer to the ground.

It starts to feel heavy, different; scary.

Unsure if you'll get hurt.

And in the time you're thinking,

You hit the ground hard.

Shattered pieces of what you once were,

Now forced to pick them up and slowly rebuild;

Waiting to fall again.

Your DNA.

Six months.

I recently heard it takes six months for someone's DNA
to no longer be in your system.

I'm not sure if it's true, but the heartbreak wants to believe
it is.

A comforting but scary thought it is.

It's nice to know that I still have a body that's tied to you.

I still have lips you've kissed, hands you've touched.

But it scares me that one day, our bodies won't remember
each other.

We'll be physical strangers.

There won't be any trace of your touch on me,

And all I'll have is the memories.

We can make it work.

I know that we can.

If you came back to me, if you just said you were sorry.

I just know we could mend what's broken.

That we could make the change and find balance again.

I can't believe that after all those times you told me

we'd make it work "no matter what",

you left for the reason of thinking it couldn't.

Melancholy.

The darkness falls over our home.

Haunted by the ghost of you, I lie there.

Paralyzed by your absence, knowing that every moment has
led to now.

I try to cleanse it, try to feel something.

Listening to your old playlists.

Wearing your old t-shirts.

Reading our old messages.

My actions, intending to make it better, make it worse.

The smiles that have faded to frowns.

The "i love you" that has become "i think we need space".

It's gone. All of it, all of us. Gone.

The ache in my chest speaks with the tears on my cheek,
your name imprinted into both.

Will I ever escape this? Will his ghost ever leave?

No. He won't.

I'll be haunted for the rest of my days,

Incapable of a cleanse.

Dancing with his ghost.

In the kitchen. In my room.

I blast music and it feels like he's here

Laughing and dancing with me.

And we're happy and in love again,

And it feels so good.

abby jeane/a delicate heart

Kinda funny how I miss his mom

just as much as I miss him :')

His cologne.

A very specific smell.

I could recognize it for miles,

like a shark with blood.

Only recently it's been in the air.

Like a random breeze, it comes fast and light

But it instantly hits me and I instantly see your name

written in my mind.

I can't escape it, I never know when it's around.

And the thing is it isn't even you, it just smells like you,

But it feels like it's you.

I smell it and suddenly I'm transported back into your arms,

my face in your chest.

I'm standing back in your bedroom with you spraying it on

your neck and saying "Okay let's go."

I'm sitting in your car reminiscing on the wonderful day we

just shared and feel sad that it's over.

His cologne.

It's just a smell, yet it takes me back to so many places and so many feelings.

And when it's around I feel excited because maybe you're around, but you never are.

It's just the memory, it's just the delusion, it's just the heartbreak of your absence.

3...2...1....*bang*.

Shots in the dark, guns in our hands

We both pulled the trigger

We both went for blood

The only difference was mine wasn't loaded

The loud sound, I shot to get a reaction

You loaded yours, and you shot me right through the heart

Walking away, very aware that you killed me

Shopping.

Sometimes I'll see something that makes me think of you.

It'll come across my feed or show up in a store

and I instantly think "I should buy that for us!" until I

remember, there is no more us.

It's just me, still thinking about you like you're mine.

I had this stupid little thought that you're thinking of me.

Maybe you are, you probably aren't;

But it's comforting to know there's always the chance that

you are.

Quick backstory.

Sitting at the table, he explains what happened to us.

Who we are, what we were, and why things are like this now.

It was weird because in my mind, everyone already knows.

They know me, they know you.

But in that moment I was hit with a moment of reality that
not everyone knows.

In fact, only a handful of people know.

And I don't know if I should find comfort in that, or if it
should sting.

abby jeane/a delicate heart

2:02 am

I wake from the dream of you and I

The paseos leading us to heaven

It's vivid and loud

Our laughs echoing in my mind

Your voice follows parallel

All dead and gone to the wind

A memory that's faded

And a dream that'll never exist

March.

The weather is starting to feel like when we first met.

2 strangers who held hands in a music video for a close

friend.

I'd give anything to go back there right now.

Take me back.

I'd trade all that I have to go back in time.

To relive the day we met.

To relive the moment in time where you liked me.

To experience the butterflies from you.

Our first texts, our flirty calls.

I'd give anything to have you look at me that way again.

When we were young and it was new,

And I was so confident that it was always going to be you.

Conversations with the mirror.

9:02 p.m.

I sit on my bed as I pretend like you're there.

You've texted me, asking to talk for the first time in months.

We meet and I speak, making you feel so guilty.

I tell you how much you've hurt me and finally receive the apology I've waited months for.

You say all the things I've wanted to hear and we decide to try again.

I love this little fantasy of mine because it goes however I wish.

Yet when I break back into reality and check my phone, it's disappointing.

There's no text.

There's no plan to meet.

It's still just me and my thoughts.

And you, unaware of our conversations.

I think about it a lot in the early mornings.

When everything feels foggy but the air is clear.

It's calm and cold, the birds sing their songs.

Down the stairs and through the hall, I think of when he'd walk next to me.

We had the whole day at our fingertips, filled with coffee and joy.

I think about it a lot in the late nights.

When everything feels clear but my thoughts are cloudy.

It's quiet and cold, cars occasionally drive by.

Staring at the ceiling lying under the blankets, I think of when we'd lie together.

Looking eye into eye, smiling as he'd pull me close.

I think about it a lot, a lot.

Whether it's in the back of my mind or the hyperfocus of my day, it's there.

And I hope it's there for him too.

Other side of the glass.

He's just so attractive

From every angle he's perfect

The left

The right

It's strange looking at him knowing that I've touched every

part of him

I've kissed up and down his neck

My hands have touched every part of his soul

But here I am

 10:46 a.m

Looking through the window at someone who's just a

stranger now

A message to the universe.

Please

I want my boy back

abby jeane/a delicate heart

I hope he's writing poetry about me too.

abby jeane/a delicate heart

Chapter Three

apoplectic.

abby jeane/a delicate heart

I just wanna know why.

Why last night?

Why now?

Why did you do it!?

You broke my heart.... Do you even care?

Was I on your mind all night?

I hope so.

God knows you were on mine.

Text me damnit!

Why won't you text me?

Do you even want to?

Man I hope I'm on your mind as much as you're on mine.

Just to see your name pop up on my phone, that's all I want;

But I guess life isn't fair.

Paranoia.

I know that you were sweating that night.

My dad walks into the room so you take me outside but it
isn't any good.

A silhouette of my sister as she peers through the window,
watching us.

Watching <u>you</u>.

We sit and suddenly my mom drives up.

You try to escape for the weekend but it travels with you.

You believe my friend to be a spy and look at her with fear,
wondering if she knows everything or nothing at all.

I'd bet you even go to work nervous, never knowing if I'll be
right next door.

I can tell you're playing it cool, always 'Mr. Nonchalant',
but let's be real.

This is eating you alive,

And I'm glad it is.

I'm not the clueless one.

It's funny because you probably think I know nothing at all,

but that isn't true.

I know a lot more than you'd even believe.

What you're up to, where you're going, how you've been.

And it isn't because I'm that psycho crazy ex,

but it's because the truth always comes to light.

One way or another, it'll get back to me.

You better keep that in mind my love.

It isn't fair.

It isn't fair that you get to go and I don't.

It isn't fair that everyone close to me gets to take a trip with

you, something that I've wanted to do for months.

It isn't fair that you get to go have fun

and I have to stay back and feel upset,

watching via Instagram stories and text messages.

It isn't fair that I didn't even get to talk to you about it

when you were the only one who had a problem with me

going.

It isn't fair. Not a single part of it is.

I really hope you understand that.

I hope he cried.

I hope he cried the night that he left.

I hope he cried days after that too.

I hope thinking about it now brings that

same body ache that started the night we crashed.

It would be so shitty of him to break my heart

and then feel a little sad.

I hope he felt awful and feels remorse looking back now.

I shed every last tear I had for him,

and I hope he did the same for me.

You can block me and pretend it didn't happen.

You can forget me and go on with your life.

Time will move and this will fade, but nothing can erase the way you felt about me.

Nothing can change the memories we shared.

And <u>nothing</u> can change the fact that you were in love with me.

My own enemy.

What bothers me the most about this mess?

I'm more mad at myself for being mad at you than I even am

at you.

You left me and I'm angry, but it never stays that way.

I think about it and it makes me quiver.

Screaming as I imagine you standing there, feeling awful.

The moment passes and then I'm left with myself, forgiving

you again.

abby jeane/a delicate heart

You grew your hair long and I cut mine short.

You blocked me from your world

and I wrote to you about mine.

You kept it all inside and I talked about it daily.

You left because you had changed for the worst,

and I was left because I was about to change for the better.

Unlucky #5.

I never wanted to be another ex-girlfriend on your list.

The fact that I am just makes me sick.

My name, now written on the list of girls who failed to keep

you happy.

And do you wanna know what makes it worse?

You promised I never would be;

And I hate that I believed you.

abby jeane/a delicate heart

I hate that your new glasses

make you look so good.

Love of my life.

A boy who used to be the love of my life is now

a cold, unrecognizable stranger.

He blocks me from his world with the same fingers

that have touched my body on the same phone

 that has my stupid face ID on it.

He goes MIA towards the same boy that introduced us

and hides away in the same house he'd bring me to each and

every day.

He speaks with the same lips that have kissed mine,

sees with the same eyes that saw me break,

and lives with the same heart that once skipped for me.

And the same brain that made him think of leaving me is the

same brain that can't think to apologize for the damage he's

done.

Unbelievable.

Unexpected dream girl.

Heard you're losing the feelings you had for me.

I'm fading from your life and you get to live all alone,

just as you wanted.

It doesn't bother me though,

because I know if you saw me your heart would skip

and your hands would shake.

You'd feel your stomach turn as the memories flood in,

and you'd be reminded of how beautiful I am.

In only 2 months?!

You replaced me like an old pair of shoes.

What was once your everything and brought along

for the adventure of your life is now just an item from the

past, thrown away and forgotten.

You found some new girl who clearly likes this new, horrible

version of you.

Part of me feels sorry for her, she has no idea what you've

become.

Another part of me is jealous that she gets your attention in

the slightest.

Either way, I know it won't end well.

Rebound relationships never last, whether you wanna admit

it's one or not.

Plus, no one is going to be able to fill the void that I left.

And you and I both know that.

A phone call on the night of Feb. 27, 2024.

"Ok well he's seeing some girl that lives down my street
and I'm publishing a book so who's really doing something
productive with their life right now?"

Deja Vu.

I bet you think about me when you're with her.

When she touches you in a way I once did, loving and
gentle.

I bet when you drive to her house you feel like you're driving
to mine.

Her street is a pathway to my little welcoming home.

I bet you make jokes and expect her to get it,

still adapted to my twisted humor.

I bet you take her places we went to,

taking the same pictures and buying the same snacks.

I bet you even blow him off to hang out with her,

unconcerned how it makes him feel.

You're relieving our life.

The same street, the same dates, a different girl.

There's nothing new.

I think he just doesn't like to be single.

Are you genuinely into her or the idea of her?

Someone new, shiny, and exciting.

Giving you attention that I used to, butterflies you once got
for me.

I never thought of you as the type to move on that fast,

but it's been clear that I didn't know you at all.

I saw you as the most honest, generous, loving person I
knew.

Recently I've seen you as the complete opposite.

You're a liar.

You're selfish.

You're cruel.

You really think moving on this fast is going to solve your
problems?

I guarantee it doesn't.

You have to own up first.

And I hope you don't drag her down too.

She doesn't deserve that from anyone, especially you.

Make it make sense.

If I talk about it too much then it's annoying and obsessive,
but if I talk about it too little then I never cared and moved
on too fast.

When I bring it up I get the sense they're tired of this
conversation but if I don't bring it up then I get asked why I
haven't talked about it yet.

I get happy about something small and suddenly I'm
"getting too excited too fast" but if I didn't get excited then
it's "rude and selfish of me"

I'm expected to move on and let go but when I do it's
concerning because "didn't he mean the world to you?"

So tell me how exactly am I supposed to be right when it
always feels like I'm wrong.

"This is considered a rebound...right?"

You never learn, do you?

The few times you've gone through a breakup

and the silence is just so loud that you need to go find

someone else.

I don't even know why I'm surprised,

this is the most "you" thing you've done in months.

Remember all those times when you told me

that you felt guilty for the girls you'd used in the past?

I do.

And that list is almost as long as your actual ex's.

You keep doing it though.

Losing someone and not knowing how to take it,

so you just talk to someone else to forget.

Will you ever learn?

If you haven't by now, I'm sure you won't.

And I think that's really sad.

abby jeane/a delicate heart

Cracked mirror

In your hand

Of Course you couldn't see yourself

You saw me,

Sitting here

I knew that you had changed.

I said that everything will get better with time,

And I'll love you even if you can't be mine

But you let each day grow darker

You may claim it's for the best

You're trying to lay our past to rest

This is a death of more than just your ego

A message I wanted to send him tonight.

"Really had to choose my neighbor huh?

Don't you think you've tortured me enough?"

Talking with my sister.

"He thinks he can escape it, he can't escape shit"

"She needs to just move on".

Trust me, I want to.

It's just a little hard when he's everywhere

and is now dating my neighbor.

He broke my heart and everything we built,

turned my life upside down and now forces me to watch

him move on.

So I'm sorry that I'm still thinking about it.

It's just hard not to when he's haunting my life.

Why'd you move on so fast?

I've thought about it for a while,

The question of if you're actually happy or just distracted.

All I know is that it can only be one of two things.

Either you're convincing yourself you're happy and moved

on,

Or...

You're a liar who never loved me the way you claimed you

did.

My revenge.

I'll be everywhere he looks, hiding in plain sight,

But he'll never be able to find me.

I'll live a life full of joy, become what I always dreamed to be,

And that'll be my revenge.

Since 10:24 am.

12 hours.

Your car was there for <u>12. hours</u>.

Get out of my neighborhood and go home.

abby jeane/a delicate heart

That picture of you sucks btw.

abby jeane/a delicate heart

Stop being so fucking dramatic.

<u>You</u> broke up with me.

Chapter Four

reflection.

A + J.

It was such a beautiful thing, you and I.

I had never felt that kind of affection, never cared for

someone like that.

Maybe one day our two hearts will be one again,

but until then I'll remember what once was,

and how much I loved you.

I loved what we were.

The way you'd make me feel, especially when you'd hold me.

I can so vividly picture how it felt.

I have hope that we'll be like that again someday, when we're older and grown.

Maybe it just wasn't our time yet, and maybe one day it can be.

11:52 a.m.

I can't help but feel that it was never,

<u>Never,</u>

Supposed to end this way.

And I feel that you feel that too.

abby jeane/a delicate heart

Brunette girl, blonde-ish boy.

When I look at the pictures,

I just see how good we look together.

I hope we get to be like that again one day.

abby jeane/a delicate heart

Though you broke my heart, I still believe in love

It may hurt to know that our love is gone

But it's wonderful to know that love is still all around

Blossoming

cryingandmanifestingshit.

I went through my private account tonight.

I found the old posts we made together and the ones I

posted just for you.

It makes me sad that we're over but seeing the memories

made me smile.

I just want to see you happy like that again.

No one's ever felt more right than you.

Maybe that's stupid to say, I'm so young.

I don't know anything.

Thinking about how it used to feel when you'd kiss me,

nothing has ever felt more right.

There was magic to us, to you.

A feeling that was different but comforting.

I hope we get to share that again someday.

Unconditional love.

The past 2 weeks have felt so long yet so short.

You've treated me like shit, but I don't hate you.

You've dragged us through the mud, but I'm not mad.

You'd think I would be too.

That I'd be cursing your name and wishing you hell,

But I'm not.

Even after all of this, I'd still take a bullet for you.

If I had to, I'd sell my soul to make your dreams come true.

If you called me crying, I'd drop everything to be there for you.

My love for you is unconditional,

and I'm confident nothing can ever change that.

Invisible String.

You've been around since I was thirteen, yet I only noticed
you two years ago.
The boy who has become one of my closest friends,
He's always been <u>your</u> best friend.
The street where we'd take my sister to playdates is the street
right behind <u>yours</u>.
In junior high, <u>you</u> sat behind me during first period,
and even had a little thing for me.
You've always been there, but I never noticed until recently.
And I can't help but think that we'll always have strings that
tie back to each other's lives.

Dreamboy.

I knew long before he was mine that he'd shatter me.

His face, something of an angel.

His voice, the sweetest melody I'd ever heard.

His touch, soft like a blanket, so warm and comforting.

When I first looked into his eyes,

I knew loving him would be dangerous.

He presented himself as such a kind, confident man,

but certainly someone who had a few ex lovers.

When he sent interest my way, I knew it would hurt.

He was something out of a dream, and I needed to

remember that.

Dreams end when you wake up.

2 years later, and here I am;

awake.

I knew I loved you more.

We used to have sweet little arguments of who loved each
other more.

A silly thing really, but it was always so pure.

The typical conversation between two lovers,

drunk on the sweet feeling of being wanted.

You'd tell me "I love you", and I'd reply "I love you more",

knowing how you'd respond.

Then you'd follow my comment with something silly but
clever, never failing to make me smile with your response.

This silly little argument made me happy, because you
caught me everytime I said it.

You always <u>insisted</u> so confidently that you would win this
argument everytime.

Did you just get tired of winning? Or tired of lying.

At least I know one of us was being honest.

January 5, 2024 at 12:44 AM.

Sometimes I lie in my bed at night and think about you.

The darkness that's fallen all over our town,

and the feeling of missing you running through my body.

Unable to remove you from my mind I wonder about how

you are, what you've been doing, if you miss me.

I wish I could talk to you, ask you questions and just talk.

I wonder if you're awake right now, and if so,

are you thinking about me?

Do you ever lie in bed thinking about me, about us?

I try to ignore it, just go to sleep before I get sad,

but I can't.

Do you go through that same cycle too?

Are you even sad anymore?

I'm so tired, but I can't get you out of my mind.

And even once I fall asleep, I know you'll be in my dreams.

The last two weeks.

What's the last 2 weeks been like for you?

What's new in your life? What's stayed the same?

How often do you think about me? Does our situation still

bring you pain?

Do you feel bad about what happened,

or are you relieved you blew out the flame?

I've tried to move on from this, act like this is all some sort

of game.

Yet everything, every song, every place;

It always leads back to your name.

abby jeane/a delicate heart

My dad once said that I "love hard" and you agreed with
him.
Somehow it was brought up that when I care, I care deeply.
A few weeks after that, you broke my heart;
Well aware that I had loved you the hardest.

abby jeane/a delicate heart

◻♡☐

It's cold today, not many people are out.

This is the type of weather that would make you say "let's go

on a walk :)".

And so we'd go and we'd walk and talk and laugh,

and you were so in love with me.

Now I go and walk, and write, and weep.

And I'm the only one still in love.

I constantly think about the night that he left me.

The things I said and the way I cried.

I think it haunts him the same way it haunts me.

There was pain in our eyes that night.

There was heartbreak in my screams.

There was loss in our last kiss.

It all vividly replays in my mind like I'm watching it on the silver screen.

After all this time I can still hear you, I can still see you.

I can still feel the way you embraced me for the last time as you placed your lips on my head.

I'm sure you've reflected on it just as many times as I have; feeling sick within your soul.

It sucks because there's no way to know if they'll ever come back.

You can search for the answer, but you won't find any results.

You can ask others, but they don't know for certain.

All you can really do is wait and hope and dream, as it all slowly fades away.

abby jeane/a delicate heart

Thank you for leaving me,

Because I wouldn't have left you.

I feel so deeply.

Whenever I look at the pictures and watch the videos I feel so much.

I smile as I remember that beautiful moment of my life, and will forever feel lucky to have experienced so much with you.

Then there's another part of me that whispers "this isn't over".

It's so silly to say but I feel as if our love story is not at an end, but on a break.

This is the part of the story where the characters are forced to look at themselves for who they are and learn what they need to be, and then return to each other.

Maybe one day our love will blossom again, but until then I'll reflect and write and work on me.

Because if we were to ever love again, I'd be sure to love you right.

abby jeane/a delicate heart

His best friend.

As I sit with him I wonder how he feels.

Your closest friend, so similar to me but different from you,

both of us balancing ourselves out with you in perfect

harmony.

Just like me, you've blocked him out too.

Pushed him away, acting cold and heartless, refusing to give

reasons as to why.

Do you realize what you're doing?

You've taken two people who care for you so deeply, and

have chosen to no longer care for them.

And the saddest part is the fear I have that you don't even

mind.

abby jeane/a delicate heart

I'm not sure what I miss more;

You or the memory of you.

I reflect back on the memories

and think about who you were.

I think about the way you treated me,

how you were always so kind and compassionate.

I look at pictures and see your smile, so warm and bright.

Your voice is an echo in my mind that breaks me down to

my soul and instantly rebuilds, polishing me with a feeling I

could never feel on my own.

I remember how I watched that version of you

slowly fade away, until eventually you were

someone I didn't even recognize.

You changed and I think deep down

we both knew that.

So I really don't know what I miss more.

You, or just the memory of you.

You or the idea of you.

You used to ask me if I loved you or the idea of you.

Sometimes you'd worry that I was lost in a fantasy that wasn't real and it wasn't you that I wanted but it was the image of you I had created in my head.

I always told you it was silly, that I loved you and every version of you.

It would scare me because I would panic and think that maybe you were right, but no.

You were always right about a lot and we both knew it, but when it came to that topic, you were wrong.

You were always wrong.

Right person, wrong time.

My friends don't believe in a "right person, wrong time"

situation.

I've seen online that apparently a lot of people don't,

because if it was the right person there would never be a

wrong time.

I just can't believe that though.

Maybe it's the heartbreak talking, but I feel that you are my

right person and that this is our wrong time.

We're young and still figuring it all out.

One day, you'll see that it's always going to be me

and I'll see that it's always going to be you.

Because we are living proof of "right person, wrong time"

I just know we are.

Poems for his golden.

I read some of your poems today.

The sacred words you wrote as we celebrated months in

love, captivated onto the page.

I wonder if you ever think about those.

The promises you failed to keep and the girl who's heart you

broke.

Pages filled with a feeling you once felt for me, and as I

re-read them I refuse to believe that they mean nothing to

you now.

Mystery.

I'm more of a mystery to you than you are to me.

Where I am and how I'm doing, you can only wonder.

Your family sees my life from afar, or at least what I share.

I don't want you knowing what's going on with me.

Silence is the best revenge, and I'm sure it's gotten to you by

now.

Change of heart.

Never thought I'd see it this way,

but you really did break up with me for me.

The past month I've seen you as selfish, heartless.

But no.

You left because you didn't want to drag me down with you.

You left to protect me.

abby jeane/a delicate heart

When we began.

I still remember how excited I felt when we first started
talking.

The way the air felt, the butterflies in my stomach,
everything.

I remember when my best friend asked if I liked you and I
lied with the biggest smile on my face.

I remember when you came home from your 5-day
backpacking trip and the adrenaline that went through my
body as you texted me.

I remember being excited to see you at school, and how
when I'd walk up you'd smirk and say "Hey, Abby".

I remember lying on my living room floor, texting you late
at night and looking forward to seeing you the next day.

I can so vividly remember the day I met your family.

You picked me up from rehearsal and I met your parents.

Your mom was smiling in the passenger seat and I heard
them introduce themselves.

When we began.

We walked back to your house from the mall and when we walked in the door I met your sister and her boyfriend, both were so nice and excited to learn who I was.

You made me the most warm, watered-down lemonade but your mom fixed it with love and I just laughed cuz I thought you were just so cute.

We sat in your backyard for the next 7 hours, talking about everything we could, an electric spark between us.

I remember how I felt once I got home, the magic of the day showered on my soul.

I still smile as I remember that perfect little Thursday, I felt so wanted and welcomed.

It feels like just yesterday it was all new.

We were falling in love, convinced it would never end.

Now we live today, where it's grown old and you've given up on falling for us, convinced it would never work.

Enchanted night.

A silk blue dress and a matching blue tie

A kind beautiful boy who says I'm his "favorite little guy"

Blackjack bets and nervous sweats

He takes my hand to dance

Lost in his eyes

Starting to realize he's about to take a chance

A car ride home and lips like a poem

I announce he's officially mine

The days that followed danced together

A new magic of him & I

Walking on a bridge with the thought "I want this forever"

Sharing poetry and making playlists

Gently seals his love with a kiss

April will always bring me back to that night

I'll reminisce on when we started

And remember his love that was my brightest light

I've accepted that you're gone,

But sometimes I really miss you being my best friend.

Old best friends.

We were always so weird and annoying together.

We had such a special bond.

So comfortable and vulnerable, not afraid to be our true

selves.

I miss our connection.

Let's fix it so we can get that spark back.

A lonely December night.

I remember lying there feeling so confused and distraught.

An endless ocean of tears flowed from a girl trying to make

sense of it all, but the more she put the pieces together the

more it hurt.

I remember how the hugs felt right after you left.

Everyone felt so bad for me, but I just couldn't allow myself

to accept that it was over.

The mumbling words from friends went right through my

head as my thoughts would linger on about you and what

could have gotten us to that point.

The night felt like an eternity.

Minutes became hours as I was paralyzed by what you had

told me.

I remember how the drive with my friends felt,

the music they played and the things they'd say in hopes to

comfort me.

A lonely December night.

I think back to that night and just remember how I
wondered if I would ever get over this, if I would ever find
peace without you in my life.

Writing this now feels weird, because I am in a totally
different place compared to then.

I still wonder if I'll ever get over it, but I have found peace
with it.

And I'm proud of myself for that.

The watermelon.

One of my most fond memories of you is the watermelon
memory.

We had just started dating.

It was a nice spring day, and we wanted something to do.

You had showed me a video of a guy launching a
watermelon and said,

"We should do that!",

So we did.

We walked over to the store and picked out the perfect one
then headed to the park.

I recorded as you threw the fruit off a bridge and cracked
jokes, intending to make me laugh.

As the days became weeks, we would still talk about that day
and always ended with "we should do that again".

It's one of our most precious memories together,

and that whole day felt like magic.

The watermelon.

I even remember when we walked over the bridge

and as I looked at you I thought,

"I want this forever"

It's now been some time since we've split,

but I still look at those videos every now and then

and laugh as I reminisce on that day.

Missing when it was all new and exciting,

and hoping that you're missing it too.

Like an oath.

It was never a secret to anyone that I was deeply in love.

I made you my whole world, and sometimes I do regret that.

My boyfriend was my entire personality,

and at the time I couldn't admit that.

You were painted onto every canvas I had.

My bedroom, my Instagram, me.

The letters, the pictures, the necklace.

I had engraved you onto every part of my life,

leaving no room for me.

Sure, maybe it was toxic and unhealthy.

Maybe I do regret doing that sometimes.

But it feels good to know that no one could ever question

how much I really loved you.

Valentine's Day.

I've always been indifferent towards February 14th.

"The day of love" is what they call it.

Couples get to celebrate their relationship as others watch from afar.

I don't want to sound like a hater,

but I hate seeing couple's get to thrive today while I'm still mourning you.

Last year you got it so right.

The flowers, the note, everything.

This year feels so wrong.

We don't even talk anymore.

So I'm sorry if I seem a little rude today;

I just hate that I don't get to celebrate the way I thought I would.

abby jeane/a delicate heart

That's just the way it is now.

He has her and I have me,

and there's nothing I can do to change that.

I just need to be ok with me.

Still blocked.

It's been 3 months and I'm still blocked.

I understand it is still fresh, but you've moved on.

You're happy now.

I've accepted that it's over and that you're her's,

But why am I still blocked?

Do you not want to see my page or do you want me to not

see yours?

I'm not upset about it, just wondering if I'll ever be let back

in.

Why are you everywhere?

I just can't escape you.

Work.

School.

My neighborhood.

You're always around.

And I see you with her and I'm so happy you're happy,

but it still hurts a part of me.

So what even is this?

Is this God's way of showing me it's time to move on?

Is it karma towards you that I just happen to always be

there?

Or is it the universe trying to push us towards each other

again?

It feels like time won't let us get too far.

We can split, but not for long.

Somehow your presence is always brought back to me.

My presence is always brought back to you.

And why?

Why are you everywhere?

Is it just a coincidence?

Is it fate?

I just don't understand why our timing is so in balance with each other.

And I wonder if you've noticed it the way I have.

From that one movie.

Every now and then, I'm reminded of all the things you used
to say.

Remembering it all hurts, but there's one specific line that's
gotten to me recently.

"I love you in every universe"

You used to tell me that little line and it would light up my
world.

When you'd kiss my ring finger and say it, I'd just melt away.

Eventually the phrase faded from your lips, but I trusted you
still meant it.

I guess at the time you did, you probably don't anymore.

Instead of loving me in every universe you've pushed me
away;

Blocking me from your world, and refusing to let me
re-enter.

His pov.

She talked to me.

I had tried avoiding her all night, and then a tap on my
shoulder and there she is,

Looking beautiful as ever and smiling.

I just broke this girl's heart two months ago, so why's she
talking to me?

I was nervous she'd say something to guilt trip me, she's
always been the type.

Yet as she spoke I stared at her and her beautiful eyes and
just thought,

"She's still just her"

The girl that had been my best friend, my golden love, my
moon and stars.

It was still just her, and that's what hurt.

She was still the girl I had fallen in love with,

But I still had the image of her teary eyes in my mind.

abby jeane/a delicate heart

So funny talking to you about my book knowing damn well,

You're the main character

My favorite ex.

You'll be the one that I sing every breakup song about.

You'll be the one that I'll miss on random days.

You'll be the one I talk about to my future grandchildren

when they ask me about the first time I was truly in love.

You'll be the one I think of when I think about a fond

memory from my high school years.

You'll be the one that I will forever wish it worked out with.

abby jeane/a delicate heart

Your new girl.

My friends say you're trying to fill a void.

My mom says you'll never find anyone like me.

Maybe they're right, but I keep thinking about what you
think of this new chapter of your life.

A new girl, a new love interest.

You've already met her family and she's met yours.

I wonder if your mom & sister compare her to me,

they've never been afraid to give their opinions on your
romantic partners.

I'm sure her family likes you, I mean how couldn't they?

You're amazing.

I truly do hope that you're happy, but not like how we once
were.

I'm sure you'll compare her to me, just as I compare him to
you.

Though you have a new girl, I'm sure I'm still in your heart.

What we had was special and no one can replace that;

Not even her.

Remembering.

There were times when I'd go over to your house

and get in my own head about things.

I'd feel nervous but then think,

"well I should enjoy this while I have it,

because one day it's going to be gone"

I guess a part of me always knew we were going to break up,

but I didn't want to admit that.

Now I think back to those times and wish I had enjoyed it

more.

Because now it is gone, and that makes me sad.

My apology to him.

If I had five more minutes with you, I'd tell you that I'm
sorry.

I know that might sound crazy of me to say, after all you left
me.

If anyone deserves an apology right now, it's me...right?

I just can't help but feel that I have a lot to apologize for too.

Looking back pains my soul for millions of reasons,

but thinking about how I treated you is a different kind of
pain.

Neither of us were perfect.

Just some young, dumb, in love teenagers,

Both just going with the flow of things.

We both made mistakes, and I want you to know

that I've acknowledged that.

I have regret for how I treated you, and I truly am sorry.

I'm sorry for the things I said that made you feel we couldn't
make it work.

My apology to him.

I'm sorry for the negativity I placed into your life

when I wasn't happy with my own.

And most importantly, I'm sorry I made you feel that you

weren't the person I wanted.

For you are all I wanted then and all I want now, and I hope

that one day, we get to try again and do it right.

abby jeane/a delicate heart

I wonder what you did with all the little gifts.

The letters, the picture frame, the guitar.

So much of your room was designed by me,

and I wonder what you still have up and what you've put

away.

I wonder where you put the necklace.

Is it in a drawer or did you just throw it out?

The picture frame of us that would sit on your dresser,

Where is it now?

Though my face is gone, my existence is still splattered all

over your walls.

And it makes me happy that you can't escape me even in

your own home.

The One That Got Away.

He has light blue eyes and paper pale skin.

His voice is gentle and his laugh is like a melody.

He cares unlike any other, and values what is his.

I've never met anyone like him before.

He's the most beautiful, wonderful,

compassionate person you could meet.

I fell for him hard.

He was my sun and I was his moon & stars.

Different but important to each other,

and beautiful when they work together.

He was my home.

A warm, welcoming cabin in the woods.

Surrounded by big, beautiful trees.

A coffee pot on the stove & jazz playing on a vinyl.

He was my best friend, my companion.

The One That Got Away.

It felt like I had known him all my life, he always felt so familiar.

I never thought I'd see the day he'd walk away.

I lost him;

And I will miss him forever.

She's never wrong.

"What you want in high school you won't want in college"

My tia told me that once.

At the time I didn't think much of it,

I never thought that it would apply to us.

Sure, I would worry, but you never gave me any reason to.

And then suddenly, you just walked away.

Maybe you just didn't want me anymore?

We can't be friends the way I thought we could.

We said we'd stay friends but as the weeks have faded into months I've come to realize that we couldn't.

We can't be friends, not now at least.

One of us would be bound to get hurt, and I know it would be me.

I would rather have you disappear from my life completely than have a friendship with you that's built off the fear of losing each other.

I would rather never speak to you again than see you everyday and not be able to give you all the love I feel so strongly for you.

So until then, I'll live and wait.

Wait until you realize that I'm the one for you.

Wait until you understand that we really can make it work together.

Wait until I'm the one you choose again.

I wonder if you compare her to me

the way I compare him to you.

abby jeane/a delicate heart

Does she know?

Imagine you meet a guy, kind and gentle.

You feel so happy when he's around and it's all so new.

He's so handsome and respectful.

Now imagine you learn that he broke up with his long-term

girlfriend 3 months ago,

And that's just the start of it.

Not only did he break up with her just recently, but she's

actually your neighbor.

And if that isn't daunting enough, you then learn that this

ex of his works next door from him and he sees her there

quite often.

And then finally, you learn that he's been ignoring his best

friend to see you.

Lucky for me, I can only imagine this, but there is a girl who

lives down my street that's living this exact life.

And do you wanna know the worst part?

I'm pretty positive she doesn't even know.

Sometimes I listen to your music.

And I don't mean this in a weird, obsessive way.

I'm not listening to your music because I think it'll

somehow bring you back to me.

I mean it in a longing, happy way.

It's just that sometimes I want to hear a certain song, a song

you showed me.

I'll play it and then I want to hear another, and another, and

another.

And then before I know it, I'm 30 songs deep into your

playlist and I'm thinking back to when you first played those

songs for me.

It makes me feel close to you, to hear your favorite melodies.

You used to brag that you had such good taste in music,

And you're totally right.

Maybe we could, maybe we couldn't.

I go back and forth in my head all the time.

Some days I'm confident we could make it work if we tried again; Other days I feel sick to my stomach because I know our story has ended.

I ask my friends hoping to receive peace of mind, and even they're in between.

When they tell me "yes" it upsets me because my initial thought is that they just want to make me feel better, yet when I'm told "no" it upsets me because how could anyone actually think we're done for good?

I'm never happy, never satisfied.

Don't tell me "yes" but please don't say "no", and don't you dare just say "maybe".

I wish I could just know, that would make this so much easier.

abby jeane/a delicate heart

It was strange but refreshing.

Somehow the "I want you to text me"

became "I hope you text me"

and then eventually it was "Please don't text me"

And I felt okay with *that*.

Everyone except you.

It was everyone except you.

The friends, the music, the way the night felt.

It was everything, except you.

I wanted you to come, hoped you'd walk in

I'd look up at the eventide sky

Wishing you'd appear

But why would you?

You weren't even invited

Yet still, I wanted you there.

I even brought you up

But of course I was met with the friendly jokes and the

devastating no's

The whole night, down to every last detail

It felt incomplete

And I'm certain it's because it was everyone except you.

Everyday I get one day closer to him reaching out.

And everyday he gets one day further

from me wanting him back.

He's a stranger.

He's a stranger but I could tell you so much about him.

I could tell you his favorite color and the things he likes to do.

I could tell you all about his childhood and family life.

I could tell you what scares him and what he finds exciting.

Hell, I could even tell you what cologne he uses.

He's a stranger, yet I know all these little details to his life.

So I guess he's just a stranger that I know all about, and that's weird.

It's an interesting thing, what we are now.

I look at you and I know I've lost the feelings,

but I haven't lost the love.

You don't give me butterflies, but I can't exactly look at you

meaninglessly.

I don't miss your texts, but sometimes I wonder if you'll

ever call.

We aren't what we used to be, but a part of me will always

hope that one day, we'll build something new.

When he was mine.

When he was mine, my life felt so perfect.

Everything I had dreamed, all in the person who sat next to me.

When he was mine, no one had ever seen me happier.

I've never liked being teased, but I'd smile so big when it came from him.

When he was mine, life was magic.

The love songs, the dances, he made life a melody.

A beautiful, magical melody.

But when he was mine, things started to slip away.

He'd ignore the conflict, I'd build something made of nothing.

It all slowly started to fade away, yet still, I knew he'd be mine.

When he was mine.

Until one day he changed his mind.

Although time has passed, I still catch myself thinking of

when he was mine,

And how even though we don't even talk anymore,

his heart will always belong to me.

He can run to her, and say words he'll never mean,

But his heart will always be mine.

And I know from the way he kissed me.

I wonder if you see my initial everywhere the way I see yours.

It's like everywhere I look, there it is.

License plates, necklaces, keyboards.

A simple little "J", so loud and bold in my eyes but

insignificant to others around me.

So please tell me, do you see my "A" everywhere?

Or am I making a deal of something that isn't actually there.

What was I ever so upset about?

I can't even remember what had me so upset

You're just a boy

A boy that means the world to me

But still, just a boy

It's as simple as that

Why'd I ever make it so complicated?

The passenger seat.

I look over and talk as if he's still there

Scratches on my dash and a polaroid picture

We drive and sing and he makes me laugh

We'll go to his house and then to mine

Touching arms from the center and a hand upon my thigh

He'll ask to play songs and take it unseriously

Laughing at his choices, looking over at me.

Yet when we arrive, I'll be the first and last to leave

For he hasn't sat in the passenger seat in months

It's all in my head, and everytime I drive, I grieve

I don't think there's been a day where I didn't think about
him.
No matter what I was doing or how distracted I was,
his name would always wonder back into my mind
His memory would appear again, and I'd miss him.

If he's reading this now.

I hope you're proud of me, that I have made you pretty impressed.

I hope you don't see this negatively, it was all in my best interest.

I hope you don't think I'm crazy or obsessive, or feel that the apoplectic chapter was too aggressive.

I hope things between us can be good again, and I hope you know that I'll always be in your corner, as a love and friend.

abby jeane/a delicate heart

This is me letting go.

I won't drive past your house or check your Spotify

I won't see you at school and watch you act shy

I won't read our old messages and wish they were recent

Or talk about your actions and how they were so indecent

I'll let it all go and stay in your past

Will stopping wondering why it all changed so fast

I'll stop hoping for an apology from you

I'll just go move on and live my life

I wish you the best and hope you're happy

Truly, I do

Breathe.

One breath in

One breath out

4 months gone to the wind

2 years of memories now full of sin

Inhale

Exhale

It's all gone away

Flashbacks to December

Easier each day

I've climbed higher and higher

Finally I've reached the top

Everything below me is left to the past

I can finally breathe, let go, and stop

Was it dramatic of me to write a book about us?

Maybe...

But it was dramatic of you to act like we never happened,

So I'd say we're even.

abby jeane/a delicate heart

I never stopped loving you btw.

Made in United States
Troutdale, OR
07/22/2024

21412769R00139